D0349576

Landforms

Volcanoes

Cassie Mayer

Heinemann
LIBRARY

www.heinemann.co.uk/library
Visit our website to find out more information about **Heinemann Library** books.

To order:
☎ Phone 44 (0) 1865 888066
📄 Send a fax to 44 (0) 1865 314091
💻 Visit the Heinemann Bookshop at www.heinemann.co.uk/library to browse our catalogue and order online.

First published in Great Britain by Heinemann Library, Halley Court, Jordan Hill, Oxford OX2 8EJ, part of Harcourt Education.Heinemann is a registered trademark of Harcourt Education Ltd.

Editorial: Tracey Crawford, Cassie Mayer, Dan Nunn, and Sarah Chappelow
Design: Jo Hinton-Malivoire
Picture Research: Ruth Blair
Production: Duncan Gilbert

Originated by Chroma Graphics (Overseas) Pte. Ltd
Printed and bound in China by South China Printing Company

10 digit ISBN 0 431 18234 5
13 digit ISBN 978 0 431 18234 6

11 10 09 08 07
10 9 8 7 6 5 4 3 2 1

British Library Cataloguing in Publication Data
Mayer, Cassie
Volcanoes. - (Landforms)
1.Volcanoes - Juvenile literature
I.Title
551.2'1
A full catalogue record for this book is available from the British Library.

Acknowledgements
The publishers would like to thank the following for permission to reproduce photographs:
Corbis pp. 4 (river, Pat O'Hara; mountain, Royalty Free; island, George Steinmetz; cave, Layne Kennedy), 5 (Galen Rowell), 6 (Philip Wallick), 8, 9 (epa), 10 (Roger Ressmeyer), 11, 12 (Larry Dale Gordon/zefa), 13 (Galen Rowell), 14 (Yann Arthus-Bertrand), 15 (Pablo Corral Vega), 16 (Yann Arthus-Bertrand), 17 (Royalty Free), 18 (Royalty Free), 19 (Jose Fuste Raga), 22 (both), 23 (crater, Galen Rowell; volcano, Larry Dale Gordon, lava, Corbis); Getty Images pp. 7 (Colin Salmon), 21 (Art Wolfe); Kraft p. 20 (Photo Researchers, Inc.).

Cover photograph of Mount Etna, Italy, reproduced with permission of Corbis/Art Wolfe. Backcover image of Vanuatu Vulcano reproduced with permission of Corbis/Larry Dale Gordon/zefa.

Every effort has been made to contact copyright holders of any material reproduced in this book. Any omissions will be rectified in subsequent printings if notice is given to the publishers.

Contents

Landforms

The land is made of different shapes.
These shapes are called landforms.

volcano

A volcano is a landform.
Volanoes are found all over the world.

What is a volcano?

A volcano is a mountain with a hole on the top.

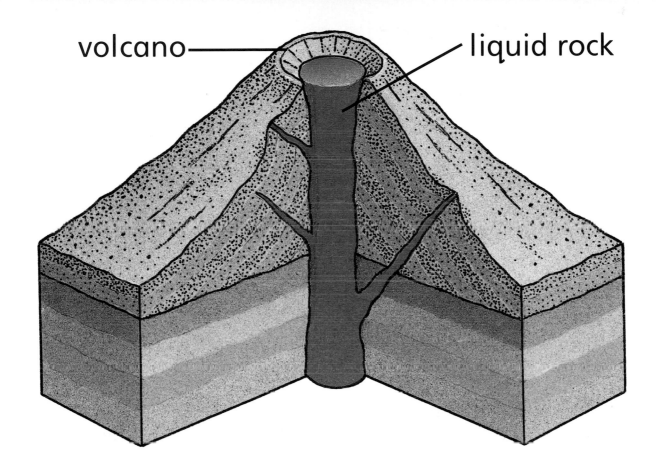

volcano — liquid rock

The hole goes down deep into the Earth. Deep in the Earth is a layer of rock which is so hot it is a liquid.

The hot liquid can rush up the hole and erupt out of the top of the volcano.

The liquid rock is called lava.

When the lava has erupted out
of the volcano it cools down and
becomes hard.

Every time the volcano erupts,
a new layer of lava is left on
the mountain.

Features of a volcano

crater

The hole at the top of a volcano is called a crater.

cone

Some volcanoes have a cone-shaped top.

Where are volcanoes found?

Some volcanoes are in hot countries.

Some volcanoes are in cold countries.

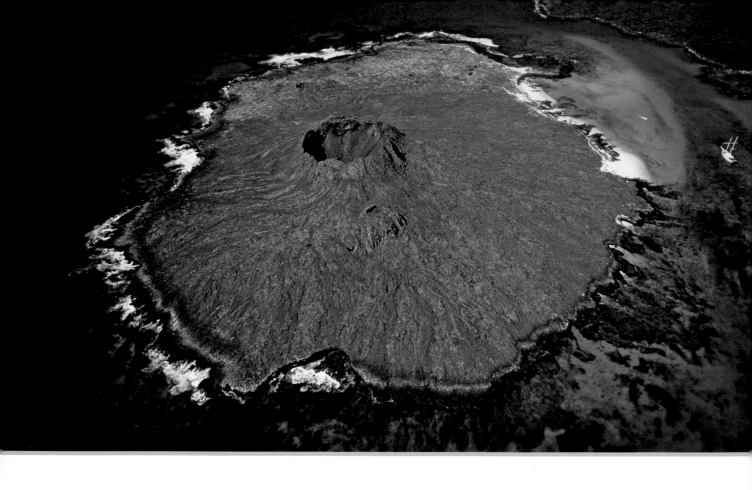

Some islands are the cones of underwater volcanoes.

Some countries have lots of volcanoes close together.

What lives near a volcano?

After an eruption, the land around a volcano is good for growing things.

Many plants grow in the soil.

Some people live near volcanoes but they have to watch out. The volcano might erupt!

Studying volcanoes

Some people study volcanoes. They check if they are about to erupt.

Volcanoes remind us that deep in the Earth there is a layer of liquid rock.

Volcano facts

Mauna Loa is a volcano in Hawaii. It is the largest volcano in the world.

The planet Mars has a volcano called Mount Olympus. It is larger than volcanoes on Earth.